Korean Americans

Scott Ingram

Curriculum Consultant: Michael Koren,
Social Studies Teacher, Maple Dale School, Fox Point, Wisconsin

WORLD ALMANAC® LIBRARY

Please visit our web site at: www.garethstevens.com
For a free color catalog describing World Almanac® Library's
list of high-quality books and multimedia programs,
call 1-800-848-2928 (USA) or 1-800-387-3178 (Canada).
World Almanac® Library's fax: (414) 332-3567.

Library of Congress Cataloging-in-Publication Data

Ingram, Scott.
    Korean Americans / by Scott Ingram.
        p. cm. — (World Almanac Library of American immigration)
    Includes bibliographical references and index.
    ISBN-10: 0-8368-7315-7 — ISBN-13: 978-0-8368-7315-3 (lib. bdg.)
    ISBN-10: 0-8368-7328-9 — ISBN-13: 978-0-8368-7328-3 (softcover)
    1. Korean Americans—History—Juvenile literature.   2. Korean Americans—
Social conditions—Juvenile literature.   3. Immigrants—United States—History—
Juvenile literature.   4. Korea—Emigration and immigration—History—Juvenile
literature.   5. United States—Emigration and immigration—History—Juvenile
literature.   I. Title.   II. Series.
    E184.K6I54   2007
    973'.04957—dc22   2006005306

First published in 2007 by
World Almanac® Library
A member of the WRC Media Family of Companies
330 West Olive Street, Suite 100
Milwaukee, WI 53212, USA

Copyright © 2007 by World Almanac® Library.

Produced by Discovery Books
Editor: Sabrina Crewe
Designer and page production: Sabine Beaupré
Photo researcher: Sabrina Crewe
Maps and diagrams: Stefan Chabluk
Consultant: Kim Park Nelson
Gareth Stevens editorial direction: Mark J. Sachner
Gareth Stevens editor: Carol Ryback
Gareth Stevens art direction: Tammy West
Gareth Stevens production: Jessica Morris

Picture credits: CORBIS: cover, 11, 17, 18, 20, 23, 33, 35, 36, 39, 41, 42; County
of Hawaii: 34; East Asian Library, University of Southern California: title page,
13, 14, 19, 21, 24, 25, 26, 27, 28, 30, 32; Library of Congress: 7, 9. 12;
Phil Nee: p. 38; U.S. Army Center of Military History: 10.

Printed in the United States of America

1 2 3 4 5 6 7 8 9 10 09 08 07 06

Contents

Front cover: Dressed in traditional costumes, Korean Americans in Los Angeles, California, celebrate their heritage with a performance of Korean dancing.

Title page: During World War II, this Korean unit of the California National Guard helped protect the United States. In the background, a Korean flag is displayed with the U.S. flag.

Introduction

The United States has often been called "a nation of immigrants." With the exception of Native Americans—who have inhabited North America for thousands of years—all Americans can trace their roots to other parts of the world.

Immigration is not a thing of the past. More than seventy million people came to the United States between 1820 and 2005. One-fifth of that total—about fourteen million people—immigrated since the start of 1990. Overall, more people have immigrated permanently to the United States than to any other single nation.

Push and Pull

Historians write of the "push" and "pull" factors that lead people to emigrate. "Push" factors are the conditions in the homeland that convince people to leave. Many immigrants to the United States were—and still are—fleeing persecution or poverty. "Pull" factors are those that attract people to settle in another country. The dream of freedom or jobs or both continues to pull immigrants

▼ This chart shows how the number of Korean Americans increased over the years since 1940. Almost 80 percent of Korean Americans have arrived since 1980.

Source: U.S. Census Bureau, Census 2000

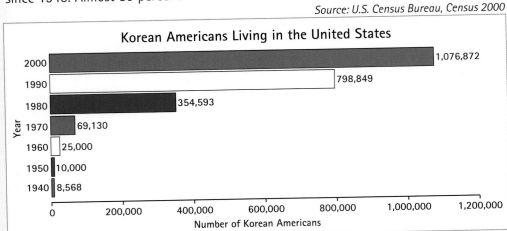

Korean Americans Living in the United States

Year	Number of Korean Americans
2000	1,076,872
1990	798,849
1980	354,593
1970	69,130
1960	25,000
1950	10,000
1940	8,568

> "In Boston, they didn't know what I was. They thought I was Filipino. And I said, 'No, no.' And they said, 'Well, in that case you must be Chinese or Japanese.' And I said 'No, I'm Korean.' And they said 'Where is Korea?' Of course, by 1950, everyone knew where Korea was."
>
> *Korean immigrant Helen Kim Griff, describing her arrival in Boston, Massachusetts, in 1947 to attend college*

to the United States. People from many countries around the world view the United States as a place of opportunity.

Building a Nation

Immigrants to the United States have not always found what they expected. People worked long hours for little pay, often doing jobs that others did not want to do. Many groups also endured prejudice.

In spite of these challenges, immigrants and their children built the United States of America, from its farms, railroads, and computer industries to its beliefs and traditions. They have enriched American life with their culture and ideas. Although they honor their heritage, most immigrants and their descendants are proud to call themselves Americans first and foremost.

A Century of Immigration

Among the immigrants to the United States between 1903 and 1907 were about seven thousand people from Korea. They traveled to Hawaii, which was then a U.S. territory. A second wave of Korean immigration began about fifty years later after the Korean War (1950–1953), in which millions of Koreans died. About fifteen thousand Koreans, mostly women and children, came to the United States between 1953 and 1965. In 1965, when U.S. immigration laws changed, a third wave of Korean immigration began. This was the largest wave—between 1960 and 2005, almost nine hundred thousand Koreans immigrated to the United States.

Economic Success

Today, there are more than one million Korean Americans in the United States. Korean Americans are one of the most economically successful immigrant groups. That success has been built almost entirely on small business ownership. Korean Americans have the highest self-employment rate among any immigrant group in the United States.

Life in the Homeland

O n a map of Asia, the Korean peninsula is a thumb-shaped landmass bordered by China, the Yellow Sea, the Korea Strait, and the Sea of Japan. Today, the Korean peninsula is made up of North Korea and South Korea.

Land of the Morning Calm

The history of Korea as a nation began in 688 A.D., when the ruler of the Shilla dynasty united three kingdoms on the peninsula under his rule. The Shilla was followed by the Koryo dynasty (918–1392). Its name was the source of the modern word "Korea," which means "Land of the Morning Calm." During this period, the Koreans developed Hangeul, a written version of the Korean language.

Koreans developed a culture that was unlike that of other countries in the region. Their original religious belief was shamanism—the belief that spirits exist in the natural

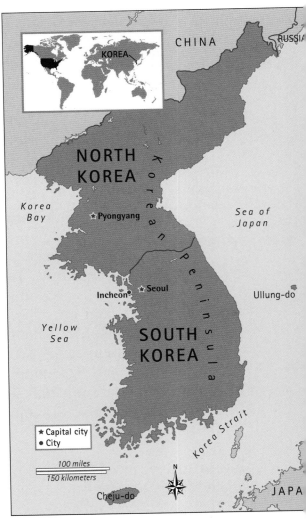

▲ Korea is a peninsula in East Asia. When Koreans came to the United States by sea, they crossed the Pacific Ocean to arrive on the West Coast.

world of plants and animals. Shamanism remains a part of Korean culture today. For centuries, Korean shamans have performed ceremonies called *gut*, in which they sing and dance to persuade spirits to increase crop harvests, cure illness, or bring good fortune.

Foreign Influence

Because Korea was a small kingdom, it was unable to keep powerful neighbors from crossing its borders. The first kingdom to exert power over the peninsula was China. Although China did not control Korea, the large nation forced trade and

▲ A busy street scene in Seoul, Korea, in the early 1900s shows crowds at a fish market. Seoul is now the capital of South Korea.

Seol

According to shamanistic beliefs, the calendar is based on the phases of the Moon. The most important Korean holiday in ancient times—and today—is Seol, the first day of the Lunar New Year. Seol usually falls in late January or early February. Families gather to eat a soup named *teokguk*, which is made with sliced rice dumplings. They also eat honey cakes called *wakwak*. Just as their ancestors did, young people gather before the eldest member of the family and bow in deep respect. As they bow, they say, "*saehae bok manhi badusayo*," which means "long life and good health in the New Year." After paying respects to their elders, families celebrate Seol by playing traditional games.

Most Koreans also consider Seol the day on which they become one year older. In this way, the Korean idea of age differs from that of Western nations. In Korean culture, a person's age is expressed in *sal*, or calendar years. A Korean baby is one sal during the first calendar year of his or her life. A child, even if it is born during the last days of the calendar year, will still become two sal on New Year's Day, when it is only a few days old.

diplomatic ties on the smaller kingdom. Chinese culture and beliefs also came to Korea. Buddhism, a religion that began in India, came to Korea from China.

The rulers of Korea began to follow the teachings of Confucius, the Chinese philosopher, in governing the Korean people. Confucius placed a high value on obedience to authority, whether it was to elders in the family or to the rulers of a kingdom. This sense of respect became a powerful force in Korea. Koreans developed a strong patriotic feeling about their country's ruler, especially during periods when Korea was controlled by more powerful nations.

In 1884, the Korean emperor allowed Westerners into Korea for the first time. Among the first Westerners to arrive were U.S. missionaries, who came to bring Christianity to Koreans. At first, the Koreans did not welcome the missionaries. By the early 1900s, however, thousands of Koreans—more than any other Asian nationals—had converted to Protestant Christianity.

> "During the war [between China and Japan] my family's . . . home was broken up and scattered. Thereafter, my uncle met missionaries from [the United States]. He said they had a Bible in one hand and a medicine chest in the other."
>
> *Emsen Charr, 1961, who emigrated from Korea to Hawaii in 1904*

Japan Gains Control

By the late 1800s, China had become weak. The island nation of Japan, meanwhile, had become a military power. Japan needed Korea's natural resources to supply its army and navy. Because China had long "protected" Korea, a war broke out between China and Japan in 1895. That war began a period of more than fifty years in which Korea was torn apart by conflict. Japan won the war against China and took military control of Korea.

Between 1902 and 1907, some Koreans emigrated to escape growing Japanese rule of their country. Koreans also left because they were encouraged by U.S. missionaries. One American, George Jones, had established a Christian church in Korea. In order to convert more Koreans to Christianity, Jones sent members of his church to the United States to be educated. He told Koreans that if they went to the United States, they would learn more about Christianity. Then they could return and bring that faith to other Koreans. Most of these first Koreans traveled, not to the mainland

Japanese troops watch Korean laborers unload army supplies in the early 1900s. When the Japanese took control of Korea, they also took control of Koreans' lives.

United States, but to the U.S. territory of Hawaii, where they hoped to find work on sugarcane plantations.

By 1910, Korea was considered an official colony of Japan. For the next thirty-five years, the Japanese governed Korea. Japanese banks and industries took economic control of the country. Koreans were not allowed to speak their own language or to study the history of their country. People were forced to take Japanese names and to convert to Shinto, the native Japanese religion. Korean peasants were forced to build factories, railroads, and roads.

Dividing the Country

When World War II broke out in 1939, Korea was still under Japanese rule. During World War II, Koreans were used as slave laborers by Japan. In 1945, Japan surrendered to the Allies, and

The Korean Sense of Han

A widely used term among Koreans is the word *han*. The word has no equivalent in English. Han comes from the Korean experience as a nation that has been conquered by foreign powers and divided by war. Korea has been controlled by China and suffered as a colony of Japan. The Korean War killed millions of Koreans. All of these events create the feeling called han. English words that have a similar meaning are bitterness, grievance, and regret. Koreans and Korean Americans say they live a life full of han when they experience an unfortunate turn of events in their own lives.

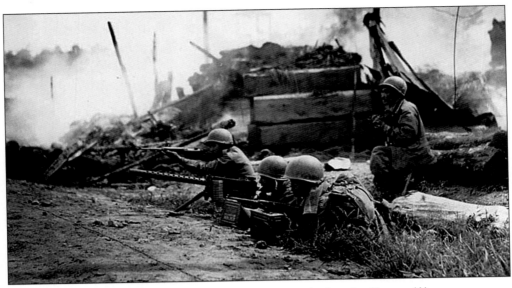

▲ A U.S. machine gun crew fires at North Koreans during the Korean War (1950–1953). The presence of U.S. troops in Korea led to a wave of Korean emigration to the United States after the war ended.

World War II ended. Within days, troops from the Soviet Union—one of the Allies—raced into northern Korea to disarm Japanese soldiers. U.S. troops had already landed on the southern part of the peninsula to take over from the Japanese there. An agreement was made between U.S. and Soviet leaders, without consulting Koreans, to divide the peninsula into two nations at a geographical line, the 38th parallel of latitude. North Korea was under Soviet control. South Korea was under the control of the United States.

The Korean War

Koreans were, once again, caught between two powers. Instead of Japanese and Chinese armies, U.S. and Soviet forces opposed each other on Korean land. In early 1946, the Soviets placed a communist government in power in North Korea. In June 1950, North Korea invaded South Korea in an attempt to spread communism to the entire peninsula.

This invasion led to the Korean War of 1950 to 1953, a war that killed more than four million Koreans—10 percent of the population of both countries. More than three hundred thousand U.S. troops fought in Korea, too, and more than fifty thousand of them died. In 1953, North Korean forces finally retreated north of the 38th parallel. Although the two nations agreed to a cease-fire, the war has never officially ended. Since 1953, the United States has kept between thirty and forty thousand troops stationed in South Korea.

The Korean War led to the second wave of emigration. Thousands of Korean women married U.S. servicemen who fought in the war or who were stationed in South Korea after the war. In addition, several thousand Korean children who had lost their families during the Korean War were adopted by U.S. families.

The Tension Continues

The third wave of Korean emigration, which began in the mid-1960s, was by far the largest. Many third-wave emigrants were from the upper and middle classes of South Korea. They left their homeland for several reasons. The economy was still weak from years of war. Opportunities for work seemed greater in the United States. Many South Koreans were also worried that tensions between North and South Korea would again erupt into war.

Hanbok

One aspect of traditional culture in Korea that has recently become popular in the United States is the traditional Korean clothing called *hanbok*. Hanbok is a brightly col-ored, two-piece cotton outfit worn by men and women. Men wear *baji*, or pants, and *jeogori*, a type of jacket. Women wear a long skirt, called *chima*, as well as a jeogori. All clothing is tied with cords or belts. Both men and women wear *durumagi*, or overcoats, in the colder weather. Men also wear a traditional circular, broad-brimmed, horsehair hat called a *gwanmo* or *kat*.

▲ Korean American dancers wear a colorful version of hanbok during a street performance in Los Angeles, California.

Emigration

L eaving Korea was a difficult decision that divided families and changed lives forever. By 1900, Koreans had suffered from the war between China and Japan that was fought in their country. Although oppressed and enslaved in their own land by the Japanese, emigration to a strange land presented a huge challenge for Koreans.

Preparing to Leave

In the early 1900s, Koreans who wished to emigrate left by steamship at the main port of Incheon, where huge Japanese battleships sat in the harbor. In order to emigrate, Koreans had to pay a fee of about $1 (about $100 in today's money) to the Korean government for a passport. Next to the passport office was the office of the Hawaiian Sugar Planters' Association. A sign in Hangeul offered to pay $15 (about $1,500 today) a month to anyone who went to Hawaii to work. Workers would receive housing, free medical care, and Sundays off. To help in recruitment, the association offered to loan Koreans enough money to pay for the journey.

Another person—the American missionary George Jones—also

◀ The two churches rising over the city of Seoul in the background were built by missionaries from Europe and the United States. Through their churches, U.S. missionaries converted Koreans to Christianity and then helped them emigrate to the United States.

helped Koreans emigrate. His church in Incheon was next to the recruitment office. Jones wrote letters that introduced Korean Christians to missionaries in Hawaii.

First to Hawaii

On December 28, 1902, the steamship *Gaelic* sailed out of Incheon, headed for Hawaii. On January 13, 1903, the *Gaelic* arrived in

Picture Brides

The Korean immigrants who emigrated to Hawaii and the U.S. mainland after 1907 were primarily female relatives or wives of workers already there. Others, however, were what came to be known as picture brides.

Arranged marriages were usual at the time in Korea and other Asian countries. By the early 1900s, photography was widespread enough that immigrant workers could send photographs to a matchmaker in Korea. The matchmaker then used the photograph to arrange a match with a young woman. The woman's family and the matchmaker eventually agreed on a husband. The bride-to-be would then be sent to the United States to marry the man chosen for her. More than nine hundred picture brides left Korea to travel to Hawaii or to the U.S. mainland between 1910 and 1924.

Some immigrant workers, however, sent photographs taken years earlier, or even false photographs, to Korean matchmakers. Such photographs made the grooms appear younger or more handsome than they actually were. One picture bride remembered: "He came to the pier, but I see he's really old. . . . He was forty-five years old, twenty-five years older than I am. My heart sunk." Nevertheless, by the time the picture brides discovered the truth, they had no choice. The contracts they had signed obligated them to marry the men chosen for them.

▲ Newlyweds Yung Ho Yoon (left) and Doyen Kim Yoon (right), in San Francisco, California, in 1915.

Honolulu, Hawaii, carrying fifty-six men, twenty-one women, and twenty-four children. Of these first emigrants, more than fifty had been converted to Christianity by Jones.

After the *Gaelic*, several ships carrying Korean immigrants left for Hawaii each month. Between 1903 and 1907, more than seven thousand Koreans, mainly men, emigrated to Hawaii. Many of these Koreans had been converted to Christianity in Korea. It was not unusual for them to convert fellow passengers during daily religious services held on the journey across the vast Pacific Ocean.

The Exclusion of Koreans and Other Asians

The first wave of Korean immigration ended abruptly in 1907. That year, U.S. and Japanese leaders signed a pact called the Gentlemen's Agreement. Under the agreement, Japan agreed to prohibit male laborers from emigrating to Hawaii or the U.S. mainland. In return, the United States agreed to allow Japan to send over the families of workers already in the United States. This agreement affected Korea because it was a colony of Japan, and the United States considered Korean immigrants to be Japanese.

Two other laws in the 1900s also affected Korean immigration. The Immigration Act of 1917 said all adult immigrants had to be able to read and write. It also banned immigrants originating from a specified zone, which covered most Asian countries. In 1924, a new immigration law barred the immigration of anyone who did not qualify for U.S. citizenship—once again, this included Koreans.

▶ This immigration identification card was issued to Kim Sung Nak in 1937. It states his nationality as Japanese, although he was actually Korean. His country of birth is shown as Chosen, which was the official name for Korea under Japanese rule.

Traveling by Air

Following World War II and the Korean War, most Korean emigrants were brides of U.S. servicemen or orphaned and abandoned children. Later emigrants, instead of spending weeks at sea, flew to the United States by airplane in less than a day.

The trip may have taken less time, but it was no easier. The military brides were leaving their own families to travel with their husbands to a new country. Few traveled with other Koreans. Most spoke very little English.

Some of the children flying to new lives with families in the United States were too young to understand what was happening to them. Others who were a little older knew they were leaving behind their brothers and sisters to join American families and take American names.

A New Kind of Emigrant

After 1965, the Koreans who emigrated also traveled by airplane. Communist-controlled North Korea did not allow its citizens to emigrate to the United States. The Koreans who left for the United States, therefore, were all from South Korea. South Korea was still rebuilding from years of war. Millions of South Koreans had moved to the cities, especially Seoul, the nation's capital, to look for work. Many were educated, but they had found little opportunity for professional employment. Others went to the United States because they had relatives already there. Under new immigration laws, family ties were an important advantage to those seeking the opportunity to live and work in the United States.

The third wave of Korean emigrants was much more familiar with the United States than those who went in earlier times. Radio and television broadcasts from the United States had appeared in South Korea since the first U.S. troops arrived. After the war, U.S. companies in South Korea employed Korean workers, while other Koreans worked at the huge U.S. military bases. In the 1970s, one of the most popular books in South Korea was titled *Day and Night of Komericans: A Visit to Korea in the United States*. The book explained how Koreans could prepare for a new life in the United States. Leaving their homes was difficult, but the third wave of Koreans usually knew someone in the Korean American community. Although few spoke English, most of the later emigrants also had at least some idea about the American way of life.

CHAPTER 3

Arriving in the United States

Koreans who emigrated from their homeland in the early 1900s left with dreams of *miguk*. This is the Korean term meaning "beautiful land" that Koreans used for America.

Arriving in Hawaii

The first wave of Korean immigration occurred during a period when other immigrant groups from Asian countries were also coming to the United States. For most of these groups—Japanese, Filipinos, Koreans—the destination was not the mainland of the United States. Instead, it was the sugarcane plantations of Hawaii.

Koreans who immigrated to Hawaii in 1903 were coming to U.S. territory, but they were not actually in one of the states. Hawaii did not become a state until 1959.

U.S. Restrictions on Asians

The Koreans who arrived to work on plantations were allowed to live and work in the United States and its territories, but they were not considered citizens. Instead, they were known as resident aliens. Koreans and other Asians, however, were denied some basic rights other aliens received. Immigrants from Europe could apply to become citizens under the process known as naturalization. Because of their race, resident aliens from Asian countries were prohibited from becoming naturalized U.S. citizens. They were termed "aliens ineligible for citizenship." Laws excluding Asians from U.S. citizenship stayed in place until the mid-1900s.

Coming to the Mainland

Although a few hundred Koreans had immigrated to California by 1905, most Korean immigration to the mainland of the United

States occurred between 1907 and 1920. Beginning in 1910, most Asian immigrants to the West Coast of the United States entered the United States at San Francisco, California. As soon as a ship carrying immigrants arrived in the city, the passengers were separated by nationality. Europeans and travelers with first- or second-class tickets would be processed on the ship and allowed to disembark and enter the country. Asians would be ferried to Angel Island, the largest island in San Francisco Bay, where they would be processed for entry to the United States.

Facing a New Culture

When the first wave of Korean immigrants faced difficulties in Hawaii and in California, they could at least turn to fellow Koreans

Angel Island

The Angel Island station in San Francisco Bay was a facility built to process immigrants as they entered the United States. When immigrants arrived, men were separated from women and children, and all were given complete medical exams. This was a deeply embarrassing experience for Koreans, because Asian medical practice did

▲ The detention center on Angel Island now houses a museum of Asian immigrant history.

not include removing clothes in front of strangers or being poked with metal instruments. After examination, the immigrants were then sent to the detention center, which was little more than a prison building. There, they awaited questioning by the Board of Special Inquiry. During this time, immigrants lived like prisoners. Living conditions were terrible, and the food was barely edible. In 1910, Luther Steward, acting commissioner for the Immigration Service in San Francisco wrote of the dormitories: "If a private individual had such an establishment, he would be arrested by local health authorities."

▲ Yoong Soon Morgan immigrated as the bride of Sergeant Johnnie Morgan. In 1952, she gave birth to the first baby born in the United States to a Korean war bride and U.S. soldier.

for support. This was not true for a later wave of Korean immigrants, who began to arrive in the United States in the 1950s. From 1950 to 1964, about fifteen thousand Koreans arrived in the United States. Of that number, about 6,500 were military brides, women married to U.S. servicemen who had been in Korea during the Korean War. Military brides continued to come in later years, too, because there were still thousands of U.S. servicemen in South Korea. Many of these women faced lonely and difficult years on their arrival in the United States. Some settled on or near military bases with no other Korean Americans nearby. Most hardly spoke English and knew very little about U.S. society.

Korean children who were orphaned or abandoned during the Korean War were also part of the second wave of immigration. More than five thousand of them came between 1950 and 1964. Older children arrived in the United States with little or no knowledge of the English language or U.S. culture. Many children were

"My [adoptive] parents were told that my name was Kim Sul Ja. . . . On all of my papers I was always referred to as Kim Sul Ja. I . . . learned that I am not the person that I thought I was. I was Kim Young Suk and there was a Kim Sul Ja at the orphanage who was to be adopted and who never did get adopted. . . . My adoption was called adoption by picture . . . I'm pretty confident the picture that my mother circled wasn't me, but the real Kim Sul Ja."

Kim Clark, who returned to Korea in 2005
for the first time in fifty years

infants who would grow up in U.S. society with no memory of their first homes.

Students Who Stayed

The remaining Korean immigrants arriving between 1950 and 1965 came as students to study at U.S. universities. After completing their studies, most of these students received visas that allowed them to work in the United States. After 1952, a new law—the McCarran-Walter Act—allowed Asians living in the United States to become citizens. When their visas expired, many Korean students followed a process of registering as aliens, then becoming naturalized citizens.

> "Many Koreans who came to the United States as students between 1950 and 1964 currently have professional occupations in the United States, including teaching positions at colleges and universities."
>
> *Dr. Pyong Gap Min, professor of sociology at Queens College in New York City*

The Third Wave

In 1965, with the new Immigration and Nationality Act, Congress overturned U.S. policies that had kept the United States closed to most Asian immigration for forty years. Immigrants with college education and professional skills in fields such as medicine or science were welcomed to the United States. So were the family members of naturalized citizens. These new immigrants became the third and largest wave of Korean immigrants.

▶ Many Korean Americans eventually became U.S. citizens. This document of citizenship was issued to Hazel Yoon in 1953. She had come to the United States many years before and lived there as a resident alien.

19

CHAPTER 4

The First Korean Americans

The experience of the first Korean Americans, those who arrived in Hawaii before 1907, was very different from that of later generations. Employed as workers on sugarcane plantations, many of them felt as if they were little more than slaves.

Harsh Working Conditions

The conditions under which the earliest immigrants worked were very harsh. The fact that their supervisors in the fields spoke only English, which most of the workers did not understand, made matters worse. Plantation workers were awakened at 4:00 A.M. and were in the fields by dawn. They labored cutting sugarcane under a blazing sun until dark. The *luna*, a white supervisor, rode among the workers on horseback carrying a whip to use on anyone who did not work fast enough. Korean American workers received about $15 (about $1,500 now) a month. Living expenses were about $8 ($800) a month. Koreans who hoped to escape the poverty of their homeland ended up only slightly better off in Hawaii.

▼ In the early 1900s, sugarcane plantation workers in Hawaii cut the long stalks by hand and gathered it for processing. They often worked from before dawn until after dusk.

Workers' Councils

Korean Americans were among the first immigrants to organize themselves into official groups once they came to a particular sugarcane plantation. Any plantation with more than thirty Koreans created a *tonghoe*, a Korean word that means "council." A *tongjang*, or chief, was elected once a year to head the council. The role of the council was to maintain order among the Korean workforce and to punish any Koreans who did not follow the agreed-upon community standards. The council also appointed a group of men called the *kyong'chal* to act as police. These men not only arrested Koreans who had broken community law, but also protected Koreans who were in disputes with members of other immigrant groups.

The Role of the Church

Religion greatly influenced the Korean immigrants. About half of the first Korean immigrants were Christian Protestants. Within months of their arrival in Hawaii, Korean American Methodists had organized Sunday services. By 1905, Korean Americans founded a Korean Episcopal church there. And by 1910, Korean American Methodist churches had also been established in several Californian cities, including Los Angeles and San Francisco.

As well as providing weekly religious services, churches served Korean American communities in other ways. The churches set up Korean-language schools that taught Korean history and culture to Korean American children. In addition, churches became meeting

▶ These Korean American students attended a Korean language school in 1926. They learned to speak Korean and write Hangeul, and they studied Korean history because their parents wanted to keep their heritage alive.

places for political groups that were organized to help free Korea from the iron grip of Japanese control.

Going Back and Moving On
Despite community and church support, many Koreans found life on the sugarcane plantations unbearable. More than two thousand first-wave immigrants—or about 30 percent of the total—returned to Korea. Other first-wave immigrants moved to Hawaii's cities, mainly to Honolulu. There, Korean Americans discovered a new economic opportunity—owning a small business.

New Opportunities
By 1910, a number of Korean American-owned businesses had been established in Hawaii. Most of these were stores that sold food or general items. Some also made and sold shoes, clothing, and furniture. These businesses made little money, and they required long, hard hours of work. For most Koreans, however, anything was better than working on the plantations. By 1930, about 90 percent of the Korean immigrants who stayed, or their descendants, had left plantation life in Hawaii to run businesses.

The Dream of Independence
Under Japanese rule, children born in Korea were given Japanese names and grew up speaking Japanese. For Korean Americans, the loss of Korean culture and language was heartbreaking. Several groups formed in the United States to fight for Korean independence. Kun Min Hur, the Korean National Association, was formed on the mainland to maintain Korean culture and resist Japan. In Korean American churches, children were taught to read and write Hangeul so the Korean language would not be forgotten. More than twenty Korean-language newspapers were published in the United States.

In 1912, Pak Yong Man established the Korean Youth Corps in Nebraska. This voluntary youth program offered military training in the farming community of Hastings. At about the same time, Syngman Rhee, a thirty-five-year-old student, earned his degree from Princeton University in New Jersey. Rhee gave speeches in several U.S. cities, explaining the Korean dream of independence to Americans. These two men, Pak and Rhee, became the leaders of an independence movement among Korean Americans in the United States.

> My mother didn't get
> [h]ere until about 1915.
> [Sh]e had those early
> [ye]ars . . . where the
> [Ja]panese had taken
> [o]ver, and she had to
> [le]arn Japanese. She
> [ha]d to bow to them. . . .
> [Fo]r her . . . these were
> [in]vaders who had come
> [an]d taken their land."
>
> *Helen Kim Griffin,*
> *whose mother came to*
> *Hawaii as a picture*
> *[br]ide, speaking in 2003*

The first wave of Korean immigration lasted just four years. In 1907, Koreans were included in the Gentlemen's Agreement between the United States and Japan that prohibited further immigration to the United States. This agreement ended most Korean immigration to the United States for forty years, although picture brides arrived until 1924.

The Gentlemen's Agreement, however, did not prevent Korean Americans in Hawaii from traveling to the U.S. mainland. Once they reached the mainland, most Korean Americans stayed in California, but some traveled farther east across the United States.

Prejudice on the Mainland

On the U.S. mainland, most white Americans knew little about Koreans or Korea. In the first two decades of the twentieth century, laws against Asian American immigrants—including Koreans—were passed at local, state, and national levels. Korean Americans in the mainland United States became victims of the prejudice and hostility directed against all Asians.

In 1905, the Asiatic Exclusion League (AEL) was formed in California. The goal of the AEL was to prevent more Asian immigrants from coming from Hawaii to the mainland. The AEL also tried to segregate Asians already in the United States from white Americans.

▶ Syngman Rhee first went to the United States in 1904. He rose to prominence as a campaigner for Korean independence and was president of South Korea from 1948 to 1960. Rhee then returned to Hawaii, where he had lived as a young man and where he died in 1965.

Under pressure from the AEL, for example, the San Francisco Board of Education ruled in 1906 that all Asian students should join the Chinese Americans at the segregated Oriental School that had been established in 1884. There were just twenty-two Korean American students in San Francisco public schools at that time, none of whom spoke Chinese or shared Chinese culture.

Farming in California

As with the immigrants to Hawaii, the first Koreans to come to the mainland were mostly Christian. In 1912, Korean Americans established churches in Reedley and Dinuba, California.

Most of the early Korean Americans on the U.S. mainland worked as servants or as farm workers, mainly on farms that grew rice. Some Korean Americans were able to save enough of their earnings to rent farmland of their own. By 1917, Korean immigrant Kim Chong-nim had become known in California as the "Rice King." He had more than 2,000 acres (800 hectares) of land under cultivation and had become relatively wealthy. Other Korean Americans operated profitable orchards, plant nurseries, and sugar beet farms.

The farming ability of Korean Americans and other Asian Americans drew the attention of white lawmakers. With efficient

▲ The congregation of the Korean American church in Dinuba, California—one of the first Korean American churches on the U.S. mainland—poses in 1930. The Korean flag is displayed on the right.

▶ A Korean American farmer and his son work in the family fields in California in the early 1900s.

farming methods, Korean Americans were able to turn dry, seemingly useless land in California's Central Valley into fertile farmland. White farmers and anti-immigrants now wanted to keep that land from aliens.

Anti-Immigrant Laws

In 1913, the first anti-Asian law to take effect statewide was passed in California. It was the Webb-Hartley Law, also called the Alien Land Law. This law said that "aliens ineligible to citizenship" could rent land for only three years. It barred aliens from purchasing any land in the future. Although the law did not mention Asians by name, "aliens ineligible to citizenship" included Korean Americans, who were barred from becoming U.S. citizens. Other laws, also using the term "aliens ineligible for citizenship," were passed by the California state government. These laws created difficulties for small businesses owned by immigrants, many of whom were Korean American.

In 1924, Congressman Albert Johnson, chairman of a government immigration committee, became the leader of the anti-immigration movement in Congress. Johnson wrote the Immigration Act of 1924, which

The First Mainland Community

The first Korean settlers made their homes in Reedley, California, and in nearby Dinuba, where they found work in the farming and fruit-packing industries. Reedley, a small town in the Central Valley, is nicknamed the "Fruit Basket of the World." More fruit is shipped from the area's huge orchards than from any other place in the United States. In 1905, the small town became home to the first Korean American community on the United States mainland. Among the people buried in the town cemetery are Harry S. Kim and Charles H. Kim, the area's first Korean business owners in the early 1920s. Harry S. Kim and Charles H. Kim established a business that operated orchards, nurseries, and a packing plant. Charles H. Kim is also credited with developing the nectarine, which resembles a peach but has a smooth skin.

▲ A grocery store owner in Whittier, California, poses for a photograph in 1925. At the time, anti-immigrant laws in California restricted Korean Americans in what they could do and where they could live.

ended most immigration to the United States. The act specifically that no Asians would be allowed to immigrate.

Close Communities

At this time, there were slightly more than eight thousand Korean Americans, many of them in southern California. Because of the anti-immigrant attitudes, immigrant groups often settled in closely knit communities. In the 1930s, several hundred Korean Americans in Los Angeles, California, settled in the city's South Central district.

Korean Americans and other Asian Americans in Los Angeles faced employment restrictions and housing segregation. Many Korean Americans chose to start their own businesses, not only because it was hard to find jobs, but also to avoid the racist attitudes they faced when working for and dealing with white people. They operated small businesses, such as barbershops and rooming houses, that served people who were not allowed to use "white-only" facilities. By the end of the 1930s, Korean Americans owned more than sixty small businesses in the Los Angeles area.

Two Wars

On December 7, 1941, Japanese forces attacked the United States at Pearl Harbor, Hawaii. The next day, the United States declared war on Japan and entered World War II. Korean Americans hoped that a U.S victory in the war would bring independence to Korea. Many volunteered to join U.S. forces. At first, Korean Americans were treated as "enemy aliens" because they were considered Japanese. In 1943, however, the U.S. government agreed to allow Korean Americans to serve in the armed forces. Young Oak Kim, the son of Korean immigrants, became the first officer from any ethnic minority in U.S. history to command an army combat battalion. He led a force of Japanese Americans and Korean Americans in key battles during the war.

Unfortunately for Koreans and Korean Americans, the end of World War II did not bring independence to Korea. Instead, it brought troops from the two most powerful nations in the world—the Soviet Union and the United States—onto the Korean peninsula. In 1950, most Americans became aware of Korea for the first time when North Korea invaded South Korea. The Korean War lasted for three bloody years. This war and its aftermath created the second wave of Korean immigration.

War Brides

Although U.S. immigration laws had barred all Asian immigration in 1924, the War Brides Act of 1946 permitted U.S. soldiers who married women while stationed in foreign countries to bring their wives to the United States. Unlike the Korean women who came in

▲ In 1944, First Lieutenant Young Oak Kim received a Silver Star for his heroic actions during World War II.

"I am the only one in my class who went to America before this holocaust happened. I returned to Korea in 1973, and my classmates held a reunion for me . . . sixty out of one hundred died or vanished fighting for both sides. . . . I was reminded of the American Civil War, brothers fighting brothers."

Journalist K.W. Lee, 2003

the first wave, these war brides did not settle in communities with other Korean immigrants. The war brides had a very different experience from the picture brides who had arrived in earlier years. Instead of being part of Korean American communities, they joined non-Korean American families, often on or near military bases. Some Korean American war brides had lonely lives, accepted neither by white Americans nor by Korean Americans. Others managed over time to form their own networks.

The War Brides Act provided a legal way for Korean immigrants to enter the United States. The McCarran-Walter Act, passed in 1952, was even more important. This law gave Asian Americans the right to become U.S. citizens and to bring in family members. Together, these laws would later contribute to a new wave of immigration.

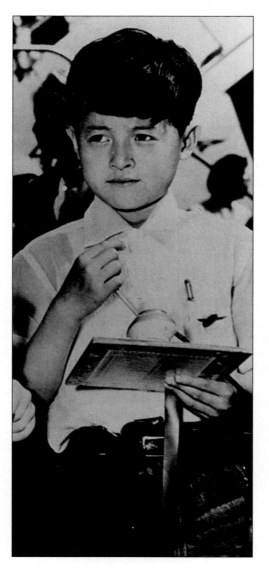

Korean Children

Few images from the Korean War created more sympathy in the United States than those of the millions of Korean children who were orphaned and abandoned in the bloodshed, destruction, and famine. Some of them, known as Amerasians, were the children of U.S. soldiers who had since left Korea. Many Amerasians were rejected by their Korean families and ended up in orphanages.

Photographs of orphaned and abandoned Korean children began to appear in U.S. newspapers and magazines during the early 1950s. Television

◀ A seven-year-old orphan from Korea arrives in a strange world to join a new family in 1955.

showed newsreels of Korean orphans on news broadcasts across the United States.

In 1955, an act of Congress allowed Bertha and Harry Holt, a couple from rural Oregon, to adopt eight South Korean orphans. The Holts soon set up an organization that specialized in the adoption of South Korean children through local churches.

Growing Up in a Different Culture

The people who adopted Korean infants and children were usually white, middle-class, Protestant Americans. Some African American couples also adopted Korean children. Most were children whose fathers had been African American soldiers. The adoption of South Korean children continued and increased in the 1970s and 1980s, long after the war. Experts estimate that between 1955 and 1977, about fifteen thousand Korean children were adopted by Americans. Today, more than one hundred thousand Korean adoptees (about 10 percent of the Korean American population) live in the U.S.

Adopted Korean children were given American names and raised in communities that had no Korean culture. Most grew up with no connection to Korea or even to other Korean Americans. The adoptions continue today—about two thousand Korean children are adopted every year by people from other countries.

Between Two Worlds

In 1999, nearly four hundred Koreans who were adopted between 1955 and 1985 assembled in Washington, D.C. This event was called the "Gathering of the First Generation of Adult Korean Adoptees." Korean Americans came from more than thirty states to talk about the experience of growing up between two worlds. One Korean adoptee, Kurt Streyffeler, said about the gathering: "Many of us were from the same orphanages. Many of us came over on the same flights. Many of us were adopted into . . . white . . . communities, mainly rural. Many of us considered ourselves white trapped in Asian bodies. The significance of this event . . . is that it is the first meeting of Korean adult adoptees . . . a chance to meet people who shared the same experience, not to have to educate people about our experiences, but to listen." Similar gatherings have taken place every few years since 1999.

CHAPTER 5

The Third Wave

B y 1965, the Korean War had been over for more than a decade. Most U.S. citizens now knew about Korea and had responded with sympathy to the suffering of the Korean people. In 1965, a new law was passed that had a dramatic effect on U.S. immigration and on the Korean American community.

The Immigration Act of 1965

The Immigration and Nationality Act of 1965 went into effect on July 1, 1968. Previously, immigration to the United States had been limited to certain races and certain nations. The revised Immigration Act allowed 290,000 people from all parts of the world into the United States each year, giving priority to those with family connections and certain professional skills. There was a quota of twenty thousand people from each nation, but the parents and children (under age twenty-one) of U.S. citizens—including naturalized citizens— were not counted in this number. This exemption meant that the number of people allowed in every year far exceeded the basic national quotas.

In the 1970s, because of the new law, more than 250,000 South Koreans immigrated to the United States. The majority

◄ In 1952, these Americans loaded a truck in Los Angeles with donated supplies for Koreans made homeless by the Korean War. By 1965, sympathetic Americans were ready to accept Koreans into U.S. society.

of Koreans who entered the United States after 1965 were educated people. In the 1980s, about 350,000 Korean immigrants arrived. During those decades, Koreans were the third-largest immigrant group after Mexicans and Filipinos. In 1988, the peak year for Korean immigration, more than 36,000 South Koreans arrived.

Settling in Cities

For many Koreans, the decision to move to cities in the United States was logical. Millions of people had earlier made the move from war-damaged rural areas of South Korea to Seoul, the capital city, and became used to city life. These city dwellers naturally settled in large U.S. cities where other Korean Americans already lived and where they hoped jobs would be plentiful. "Koreatowns" formed in neighborhoods of San Francisco, Chicago, New York City, and Washington, D.C. No city, however, had more Korean Americans than Los Angeles. There, the population of Korean Americans rose from five thousand in 1970 to 150,000 in 1980. It became the largest Korean community outside of Korea.

A Need for Medical Workers

In the same year that the new immigration law was passed, Congress passed two other laws that drew Korean immigrants to the United States. These were Medicare and Medicaid, programs providing health care for the elderly and the poor across the United States. The new legislation had a significant effect on U.S. hospitals. Many hospitals, especially those in poorer districts of large cities, needed many more doctors, nurses, and other professional health care workers. A shortage of qualified

Bringing in Families

As a result of the 1965 law, Korean American military brides—already U.S. citizens—were able to bring their brothers, sisters, and parents to the United States. Brothers and sisters who were married and became naturalized citizens would then bring over their in-laws and other family members. For example, Tomiko Ok Hui Lee, a Korean American military bride, brought in eighteen members of her family. Those immigrants, in turn, sponsored more South Korean relatives after they became naturalized citizens. It is estimated that military brides were in some way responsible for about 50 percent of all Korean immigrants since 1965.

Korean Names

Koreans do not have middle names. In the name Kim Min Ho, for example, Min is part of the first name, Min Ho. Kim, the family name, is traditionally placed first instead of last, although in the United States Korean names are often presented in the Western style, with family name last. Because of the differences between Korean and English, the same names may be spelled

differently. Some Korean Americans, for example, use Lee as their family name; others use Yi. Both mean the same in Korean. About 40 percent of the Korean American population has one of four family names: Kim, Lee, Park, or Choi. This is how they are pronounced:

Kim—"K" sounds like the "g" in *give*.
Lee—"L" is pronounced "Y."
Park—"P" is pronounced "B."
Choi—rhymes with *toe*, not *toy*.

▲ Sammy Lee is one of many Korean Americans with the last name Lee. He was born in California in 1920 and became a physician. Lee served in the U.S. Army during the Korean War. He also won gold medals for diving in the 1948 and 1952 Olympics.

professionals arose. This need opened the door for medical personnel from other nations.

During the Korean War and its aftermath, there had been a tremendous need for doctors and nurses in South Korea. Seoul National University Medical College became a highly respected school of medicine, and exchange programs with U.S. medical schools in the 1950s and 1960s also helped train South Korean doctors. The professionals needed in the United States, therefore, were available in South Korea.

When the Immigration Act of 1965 opened the door, more than thirteen thousand South Korean doctors, nurses, and pharmacists entered the United States. Many of these immigrants remained in the United States and, after a number of years, became naturalized citizens. Among Korean immigrants in the third wave, medical professionals who arrived before 1980 achieved the most economic success in the United States. They have among the highest incomes in the Korean American community.

The Language Barrier

Not all educated Korean Americans were able to enter their chosen professions. More than half of the third-wave immigrants were college graduates, but many were unable to speak English well enough to get jobs in their professional fields. As other Korean Americans had done before them, many third-wave Korean Americans opened or bought small businesses. This type of work did not require them to be fluent in English.

Small Business Owners

Self-employment became the economic path that separated Korean Americans from other ethnic groups. In many cases, the businesses were neighborhood fruit-and-vegetable markets. Studies showed that Korean Americans were ten times more likely to own a grocery store than non-Korean Americans. In southern California, Korean Americans own 46 percent of all small grocery markets and 45 percent of one-hour photo shops. In 1990, Koreans owned and operated more than 2,800 grocery stores in Los Angeles alone. Another study in New York City revealed that Koreans owned 75 percent of all fruit-and-vegetable markets—and that 78 percent of them held college degrees. Across the nation, Korean Americans own about 20 percent of all dry-cleaning businesses.

Whether they owned small businesses or worked for businesses owned by other Korean Americans, most third-wave immigrants labored extremely long hours. In some cases, both parents were at work before their children left for school and reached home long after the children were asleep.

The Chung family—Mr. and Mrs. Chung and their children, Steve and Christy—faced challenges typical for

▲ A demand for doctors and nurses developed in the United States in the 1960s, encouraging the immigration of thousands of medical professionals from South Korea.

Korean Americans. The parents were teachers in Korea who immigrated to Los Angeles, California. The father, Mr. Chung, worked as a janitor, a store clerk, and a painter. Mrs. Chung worked as a seamstress and sold sandwiches. The Chungs became discouraged about working conditions in the United States and decided to move back to South Korea. They changed their decision when Steve showed his parents a certificate stating that he had been elected president of his third-grade class. Steve and Christy both graduated from Harvard University. Steve is now a business executive, Christy is a dentist, and Mr. and Mrs. Chung own a jewelry business.

Community Tension

As the number of Korean Americans opening businesses in cities grew, conflicts arose between some Korean Americans and other minorities, mainly African Americans and Hispanic Americans. The appearance of Korean American-owned businesses in minority neighborhoods created anti-Asian attitudes. Korean Americans were seen as people who took jobs away from others. The Korean

Descendants of the First Wave

As Koreans continued to arrive in the United States and face the challenges of immigration, older Korean American communities flourished. A century after the first Korean immigrants arrived in Hawaii in 1903, their descendants made up about 5 percent of that state's population. Korean Americans became among the most educated and economically successful of all ethnic groups in Hawaii.

In 2005, the Superintendent of Education, the Chief Justice of the Hawaiian Supreme Court, and the mayor of the County of Hawaii were all Americans of Korean descent. In many ways, the success of these Americans is similar to that of other immigrant groups who have been in the United States for a century or more. The children of the original immigrants learned English as they grew up. They went on to higher education and pursued opportunities in modern U.S. society that had not been available to their ancestors.

◀ Harry Kim was elected mayor of the County of Hawaii in 2000.

▲ Korean American teenagers shop in a music store in Koreatown, Los Angeles. In the 1990s, tension grew between Korean Americans and other minorities in Koreatown.

American practice of hiring family members or other Korean Americans to work in their businesses also created resentment in areas where jobs were few. The language barrier, too, was significant in city areas, and Korean Americans who struggled to speak English to their customers were at a disadvantage.

Once again, Korean Americans had to face prejudice from other Americans. In a number of cities, tension developed into hostility, especially between African Americans and Korean American business owners. As early as 1981, a misunderstanding between a Korean American merchant and an African American customer in New York City led to an eight-week boycott of that store. In 1983, an African American newspaper, the Los Angeles *Sentinel*, called for African Americans to boycott all Korean-owned stores. In African American neighborhoods in New York, Los Angeles, and Chicago, Korean stores were boycotted.

The Harlins Case

Tension between the African American and Korean American communities in Los Angeles rose particularly high because of the Latasha Harlins case. In March 1991, Harlins, a fifteen-year-old African American girl, went into a Korean American-owned store to buy a bottle of orange juice. She put the bottle into her backpack and walked to the counter to pay for the drink. The clerk, Soon Ja Du, accused Harlins of trying to steal the bottle. Du grabbed Harlins's backpack, and the teenager punched Du in the face. As Harlins turned away, Du reached for a pistol and fired, killing the teenager. In October, a jury found forty-nine-year-old Du guilty of voluntary manslaughter. She faced more than ten years in prison. The judge, however, suspended her sentence, placing her on probation and ordering her to perform community service. African Americans were outraged.

Sa I Goo: April 29

Many Korean Americans—and even some South Koreans—understand the meaning of the term *Sa I Goo*, which means April 29 in Korean. There is no need to give a year—they know it was 1992. On April 29, 1992, Los Angeles exploded into rioting and bloodshed.

The cause of the violence was the acquittal of four white police officers who had severely beaten African American Rodney King. The verdict enraged the African American community, and mobs

▼ Flames spread through Koreatown in South Central Los Angeles during the riots of 1992. Many Korean American businesses were damaged or destroyed.

of African Americans and Hispanic Americans filled the streets, starting fires, overturning cars, and destroying businesses. The violence took place mainly in the South Central district, which includes Koreatown.

The riots killed more than fifty people, including one Korean American, and caused $1 billion worth of property damage. More than 560 businesses were destroyed. Although Korean Americans had no role in the King case, they became targets of the violence. In Koreatown, more than 300 businesses were burned and looted, and more than 2,000 Korean American businesses suffered some form of damage, totalling $400 million.

The Aftermath of the Riots

The impact of the Los Angeles riots on Korean Americans was enormous. Economically, the riots severely damaged the community. Korean American business owners continued to feel threatened. By 1996, more than 25 percent of the businesses in Koreatown had closed—businesses that were actually undamaged in the rioting. Many Korean Americans left the city, and others left the United States altogether. In 1992 alone, more than 6,480 Korean Americans returned to South Korea. This pattern continued through the 1990s.

The aftermath of *Sa I Goo* also reached South Korea. People there

Cultural Misunderstanding

Some of the misunderstandings that led to prejudice against Korean Americans by other Americans were due to cultural differences. What is considered good manners in one society is considered rude in another. In American culture, for example, eye contact is interpreted as respectful and sincere. In Korean society, however, it is considered disrespectful to make eye contact with elders or with strangers. In Korean American-owned businesses, this led to a feeling among non-Korean Americans that the business owners were dishonest because they would not look at their customers. Likewise, when taking money or returning change for a purchase in Korea, it is considered polite to put the money on the counter rather than exchange it from hand to hand. Touching strangers is considered rude. To many African Americans and Hispanic Americans who did not understand Korean culture, these actions may have suggested that Korean Americans did not want to interact with people of a different race.

were concerned about anti-Korean prejudice, and they began to lose interest in going to the United States. In addition, the South Korean economy had begun to improve. These two factors combined to cause a drop in the number of Korean immigrants.

> "Korean America was born in April of 1992. [Before that] in the Korean community, there was no interest in understanding what place Korean Americans might occupy in America. [This is] not to diminish previous generations—my parents and grandparents were previous generations. But Korean America . . . was wakened in April 1992."
>
> *Angela Oh, attorney in Los Angeles who served as spokesperson for the Korean American community following the 1992 riots, 2003*

Easing Tensions

There were some positive results from the events of April 1992. Korean Americans and other ethnic groups began to search for ways to overcome misunderstanding and ease tensions. Korean American and African American community leaders, as well as young people in Los Angeles, joined forces to ease the tension between the two groups. Such organizations as the Coalition of Neighborhood Developers, the Multicultural Collaborative, and Colors United helped to raise cooperation between racial and ethnic groups in Los Angeles.

In 1994, fifty African American teenagers from Los Angeles were invited to South Korea under an exchange program offered by the South Korean government. A number of church groups —strong forces in both the Korean American and African American communities—also organized scholarships and tour programs for African American youth.

◀ Many Korean Americans who were born and raised in the United States, such as comedian Margaret Cho, must straddle the divide between the traditions of their families and modern U.S. culture.

In the aftermath of the riots, many older Korean Americans looked for direction to the "1.5 Generation"—Korean Americans who had been born in Korea but had come to the United States as children and grown up as Americans. The Korean American Coalition, founded by Charles Kim, was created during this time to bridge the cultural gap between Korean and other Americans.

Tae Kwon Do

One of the first ways in which non-Koreans have become aware of Korean culture in recent years is through the martial art that is the national sport of Korea—Tae Kwon Do. In Korean, *tae* means to strike with the foot, and *kwon* means to strike with the hand. U.S. soldiers were the first Americans to encounter the sport, during the Korean War. In 1956, martial arts master Jhoon Rhee opened the first Tae Kwon Do school in the United States in Washington, D.C. Other teachers followed Rhee to the United States, especially after 1965. In most cases, these first teachers were veterans of the South Korean armed forces who taught Tae Kwon Do to U.S. troops during the Vietnam War. Today, there are more than five thousand Tae Kwon Do schools in cities and towns across the United States.

▲ In the United States, Tae Kwon Do students start at a young age.

Korean Americans in U.S. Society

According to the 2000 U.S. census, more than 1.2 million Americans of Korean descent lived in the United States in 2000. The number has grown since then, and there are also at least one million Koreans in the United States as students or temporary workers. The U.S. government estimated in 2000 that there were fifty-five thousand unauthorized Korean immigrants—people without visas or U.S. citizenship—living in the United States.

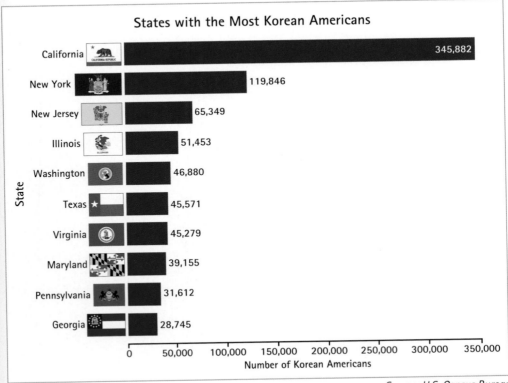

States with the Most Korean Americans

State	Number of Korean Americans
California	345,882
New York	119,846
New Jersey	65,349
Illinois	51,453
Washington	46,880
Texas	45,571
Virginia	45,279
Maryland	39,155
Pennsylvania	31,612
Georgia	28,745

Source: U.S. Census Bureau

▲ Most Korean Americans live in two states—California and New York—but Korean Americans have settled in every other state, too.

Where Korean Americans Live

In general, new Korean immigrants continue to settle in areas where other Korean Americans live, usually in cities. After Los Angeles, the cities with the largest Korean American populations are New York City, Washington, D.C., San Francisco, and Chicago. Since 1990, more than 20 percent of new arrivals from Korea have settled in the southern regions of the United States.

Going to Church

Like the early Korean immigrants to the United States, the third wave of Korean immigrants comprised a large number of Christian Protestants. While fewer than half of Koreans in Korea are Christians, more than 70 percent of Korean Americans attend Protestant churches. Today, there are more than four thousand Korean American churches across the United States.

Going to Work

The stereotype of Korean Americans at work is one of business owners and doctors. Most Korean Americans, in fact, work in factories or offices or in various service industries. The proportion of self-employed and medical professionals is still high, however.

The language barrier remains an obstacle at work. According to census information, more than 75 percent of Korean Americans speak Korean as their main language. Almost half of all Korean Americans say that they speak English "less than well."

Communities Create Barriers

Annandale, Virginia, a suburb of Washington, D.C., has more than sixty-six thousand Korean American residents. Locally, Annandale is known as Koreatown. There are more than nine hundred Korean American

▸ The Korean Korner supermarket in Wheaton, Maryland, sells groceries, including traditional Korean foods, to the large Korean American community in the state.

businesses in Annandale, which is about one-third of all Korean American businesses in the Washington, D.C., area.

Many stores and offices in downtown Annandale have large signs in Hangeul with small English words underneath. In many stores, it is unusual to hear English spoken. In some restaurants, menus are written only in Hangeul. Merchants advertise to other Korean Americans in the area's fourteen daily and weekly Korean American newspapers.

Some non-Korean Annandale residents say they feel "excluded" from the downtown area—a feeling familiar to Korean Americans, who, as a group, have suffered a century of exclusion and prejudice. Some Korean Americans have also expressed concern that

Family and Community Tradition

As Korean Americans increasingly become part of U.S. culture, many families and communities continue to honor traditions from the homeland. Among Korean Americans, it is very important to respect elders, especially parents and teachers.

▲ Korean Americans prepare to play their drums with the Hawaii Korean Farmers' Dance and Music group at a festival in Honolulu, Hawaii.

In a traditional wedding, a Korean American groom carries the bride on his back around the room to show he will take care of her. Then he carries his mother to show that, as a grown son, he will take care of her, too. Korean Americans eat traditional Korean foods, including *kimchi*, a cabbage dish that accompanies other foods. Korean Americans also prepare the traditional dishes of their ancestors for the festivals and holidays—including Seol and the harvest festival of *Ch'usok*—that are celebrated in Korean American communities. At these celebrations, Korean Americans and other Americans can see performances of ancient Korean folk music and dance. *P'ansori* is musical storytelling—some of the more epic stories can last for hours. Across the United States, groups perform *p'ungmul*, the traditional music played by percussion bands in Korean farming communities. *Salp'uri* is a traditional dance form used to ward off evil spirits. *Minyo* are the songs that people sing while working or to accompany rituals.

Koreatowns such as the one in Annandale keep Korean Americans apart from other Americans. "We have to assimilate ourselves into an American way of life and become part of the country, rather than creating a Korean community," says the owner of a Korean American hardware store in Annandale.

The Next Generation
Many Americans of Korean descent look toward the younger generation of Korean Americans to lead the way to more interaction with other communities. As the next generation grows up, it will join the 1.5 Generation in leading Korean Americans. Many of these young people show little interest in taking on the demands and risks of running small businesses like their parents. Their ability to speak English gives them a wider range of economic opportunity. A significant number of U.S.-raised Korean Americans—48 percent of women and 9 percent of men—marry non-Koreans, which shows their participation in U.S. society beyond the Korean community.

Like other groups in U.S. society, younger Korean Americans often go to live in areas where they see better educational opportunities for their children, improved living conditions, and a more diverse population. Many have settled in the suburbs surrounding Los Angeles. A number of Korean Americans who grew up in New York City now live in the suburban areas of Connecticut and New Jersey. The same is true of towns and suburbs around Washington, D.C.

One Century Later
On January 13, 2003, a century after the first Korean immigrants arrived in Hawaii, President George W. Bush honored Korean Americans for their "important role in building, defending, and sustaining the United States of America." Korean Americans have become part of the American story. The people from the "Land of the Morning Calm" have made a place for themselves in *miguk*—the beautiful land.

"My hope is that at the turn of the next century, when we are looking back at two hundred years of Korean American history, we won't be talking about Korean Americans . . . Americans will just say, 'Oh, you're Korean American, I thought you were American.'"

Mark Keam, who immigrated to Los Angeles as a child and works as a lawyer in the U.S. Congress, 2003

Notable Korean Americans

Philip Ahn (1905–1978) Korean American actor who appeared in movies and on television in the 1950s and 1960s and who is believed to be the first Korean American actor born in the United States.

Sarah Chang (1980–) U.S.-born violinist, a child prodigy who made her first classical recording at age nine.

Margaret Cho (1968–) U.S.-born comedian and television star.

Philip Jaisohn (Seo Jae Pil) (1864–1951) Businessman and doctor who came to the United States in 1882 and was the first Korean American to receive a degree from a medical institution, Columbia Medical College in New York City.

Harry Kim (1938–) U.S.-born mayor of Hawaii County who was elected in 2000–the first mayor of Korean descent in the United States.

Jay Kim (1939–) U.S.-born former Republican Congressman from California.

Sammy Lee (1920–) U.S.-born doctor and champion diver who was the first Asian American to win a gold medal in the Olympic Games.

Jhoon Rhee (1932–) Korean-born "father" of U.S. Tae Kwon Do who brought the Korean martial art and national sport to the United States in 1956.

Syngman Rhee (Lee Seung-man) (1875–1965) Korean-born political leader who was the first Korean to receive a Ph.D from a U.S. university (Princeton University in New Jersey) and went on to become the first president of the Republic of South Korea.

Hines Ward, Jr. (1976–) Korean-born son of a Korean mother and African American father who is a professional football player for the Pittsburgh Steelers.

John Yoo (1968–) U.S.-born law professor and former Deputy Attorney General in the U.S. Department of Justice.

Time Line

1903 Steamship *Gaelic* arrives in Honolulu, Hawaii.
1904 Syngman Rhee arrives in the United States.
1905 Asiatic Exclusion League (AEL) is formed in San Francisco.
1907 Japan and United States sign the Gentlemen's Agreement.
1910 Japan officially makes Korea its colony; first of the picture brides comes to the United States from Korea.
1913 California passes the Alien Land Law.
1924 Immigration Act of 1924 (also called the National Origins Act) is passed by Congress.
1939 World War II begins.
1945 Korea is divided at the 38th Parallel into two nations, Soviet-occupied North Korea and U.S.-occupied South Korea.
1947 Syngman Rhee becomes first president of Republic of South Korea; the new nation is inaugurated the following year.
1948 Sammy Lee wins a gold medal for diving for the United States at the Olympic Games in London, England.
1950 June 25: Korean War begins.
1952 Sammy Lee wins a gold medal for diving for the United States at the Olympic Games in Helsinki, Finland.
1953 Congress declares May 2 will be celebrated as Korea Day in the United States.
      July 23: Truce ending Korean War is signed.
1956 Harry Holt returns to United States from Korea with eight orphans.
1965 Immigration and Nationality Act is passed by Congress.
1992 April–May: Korean American community in Los Angeles suffers devastating losses during riots.
      Korean American businessman and Californian Jay Kim is elected to the U.S. Congress.
1994 Margaret Cho becomes the first Korean American to star in her own television show, *All-American Girl*.
2000 Harry Kim is elected mayor of Hawaii County.
2003 Hundredth anniversary of Korean immigration to the United States takes place.

Glossary

alien person living in a nation other than his or her birth nation and who has not become a citizen of his or her new nation of residence

Allies nations—including the United States and the Soviet Union—that fought against Japan and other nations during World War II

assimilate absorb or blend into the way of life of a society

boycott refusal by a person or group to do business with certain companies to protest the companies' policies

cease-fire agreement between opposing forces to stop fighting temporarily

census official population count

colony nation, territory, or people under the control of another country

communist a political system in which government has strong control and property is shared among all citizens

culture language, beliefs, customs, and ways of life shared by a group of people from the same region or nation

dynasty line of rulers, usually physically related, that control a nation for a long period of time

emigrate leave one nation or region to go and live in another place

ethnic having certain racial, national, tribal, religious, or cultural origins

heritage something handed down from previous generations

immigrant person who arrives in a new nation or region to take up residence

missionary person sent by a church to convert other people to that church's religion

naturalization process of becoming a citizen by living in the United States for a number of years and passing a citizenship test

peninsula land mostly surrounded by water but connected to mainland on one side

plantation large farm that grows primarily one crop, such as sugarcane, cotton, or tea

prejudice bias against or dislike of a person or group because of race, nationality, or other factors

quota assigned proportion; in the case of immigration, a limit on the number of immigrants allowed from a particular country

segregate keep different ethnic or racial groups separate from one another

service industry area of work that provides services instead of products; service businesses include banks, entertainment, food service, tourism, and health care, among many others

shaman spiritual leader in certain societies who is believed to have special powers

sponsor put someone's name forward and take responsibility for them

stereotype image, often incorrect, that people have of certain groups

visa document that permits a person to enter a nation for a set period of time

Further Resources

Books

Horn, Geoffrey M. *Michelle Wie.* Today's Superstars: Sports (series). Gareth Stevens, 2006.

Hyun, Sook Han. *Many Lives Intertwined.* Yeong and Yeong Book Company, 2004.

Kim, Elaine H. and Eui-Young Yu. *East to America: Korean American Life Stories.* W. W. Norton, 1996.

Stickler, Jon. *Land of Morning Calm: Korean Culture Then and Now.* Shen's Books, 2003.

Web Sites

Arirang—an Interactive Classroom on the Korean American Experience
arirangeducation.com/main/
Web site about Korean American history from the University of Hawaii

Korean Alphabet
www.geocities.com/Tokyo/Pagoda/1876/hangul.htm
Information about Hangeul, the Korean written language

Publisher's note to educators and parents: Our editors have carefully reviewed these Web sites to ensure that they are suitable for children. Many Web sites change frequently, however, and we cannot guarantee that a site's future contents will continue to meet our high standards of quality and educational value. Be advised that children should be closely supervised whenever they access the Internet.

Where to Visit

Hawaii's Plantation Village
94-695 Waipahu Street, Waipahu, HI 96797;
Telephone: (808) 677-0110
www.hawaiimuseums.org/mc/isoahu_hplantation.htm

About the Author

Scott Ingram is the author of more than fifty books for young adults. In 2004, he won the NAACP Image Award for an outstanding literary work for children for his book about the Civil Rights March of 1963, published by World Almanac® Library in its *Landmark Events in American History* series. Ingram lives in Portland, Connecticut.

Index